Pure Reason

For Nikos from Howard 2007

Pure Reason

Poems by Nikos Stangos

With an introduction and notes by David Plante
and contributions from the poet's artist-friends

Frontispiece HOWARD HODGKIN *For Nikos from Howard*, 2007

First published in 2007 in hardcover in the United States of America by
Thames & Hudson Inc., 500 Fifth Avenue, New York, New York 10110

thamesandhudsonusa.com

Library of Congress Catalog Card Number 2007901137

ISBN 978-0-500-51383-5

Printed and bound in Verona by Editoriale Bortolazzi-Stei srl

CONTENTS

DAVID HOCKNEY *Nikos Stangos. London. 21st May 1999*, 1999

INTRODUCTION

Nikos Stangos was born in Athens in November 1936. His mother was
from an old Constantinopolitan family, his father from an old Greek
family in Sosopol in Bulgaria, the ancient Greek city of Apollonia
on the Black Sea; Nikos was thus descended from both the Byzantine
and the Classical Greek worlds. He lived through the German
occupation of Greece during World War Two and the Greek Civil War
and remembered hearing, from the street below, men pushing barrows
loaded with corpses and calling out, 'Bring out your dead.' At the age
of eight, he became a boarder at the American College at Athens,
a neo-classical building that had been designed by his father, and
during the eight years there developed his vision of poetry and socialist
politics. In his teens, he became a member of the Communist Party,
mimeographing propaganda which he threw from the balconies of
cinemas, a dangerous activity, as the Communist Party was then
prohibited. His poetry, submitted at cell meetings, was criticized harshly
as being too formalistic and sexually ambiguous, and he left the Party,
keeping, however, all his life the belief in the ideals of socialist duties.

He left Greece in 1956 to continue his undergraduate studies in
the United States – first at Denison University in Ohio, and then at
Wesleyan University in Connecticut, after which he went on to Harvard
University in Cambridge, Massachusetts, for graduate studies in
philosophy. After Harvard, he returned to Greece to fulfil his military
duty. In 1965, he came to London, and was offered a position in the
office of the Press Attaché of the Greek Embassy. While in Greece,
he had been given the names of poets in London by Nanos Valoritis,
the Greek poet who himself had lived there, and among these names
was Stephen Spender, who introduced Nikos to the cultural world
of 1960s London. He and Spender collaborated with David Hockney
on a collection of translations of poems by Constantine Cavafy, with
etchings by Hockney in the spirit of Cavafy.

ANDREW LORD *'The memory of you at one particular moment, at another particular moment and a third particular moment.' For Nikos Stangos*, 2007

In 1967, with the takeover of Greece by the colonels, he left the Embassy, joined demonstrations against the dictators, and was granted permanent residence in the UK. He was interviewed by the then aged Allen Lane, the founder of Penguin Books, and was taken on as editor of poetry, art and architecture, theatre and cinema, and philosophy. Following the death of Lane, in 1974 he left Penguin Books to join Thames & Hudson, one of the very few independent publishing houses left that sustained originality and high standards. Enjoying the mutual respect and enthusiasm of the then chairman of Thames & Hudson, Eva Neurath, and the present chairman, Thomas Neurath, he was made a director. The many acknowledgments in the books he commissioned and edited show the high esteem in which his writers held him. Before his death, he completed a long poem in Greek, called 'Τί ἐστιν ἀλήθεια;', or 'What is Truth?' He died in London in April 2004.

Though he was editor of poetry at Penguin Books from 1967 until 1974, and established himself as an enthusiastic and innovative (a favourite expression of his) publisher of poetry, he was without ambition for his own writing. All the poems in this volume are published posthumously.

KEITH MILOW *British Museum*, 2006

THE PURITY OF DURATION

And I will try to think
Of the duration
Pure like the chest of
A young man
Not the beginning or end
But the pure duration
Like the chest of a young man
Which is, was, or has been
Will be perhaps:
To be is to be
Pure like the chest of a young man
In a dark moonless night
When the solidity of darkness and the chest
Construe one reality:
The purity of duration
And the chest of the young man
That I will try to think about
Until dawn.

DAVID HOCKNEY *Nikos Stangos. London,* 1999

THE DEFINITION OF THE GOOD

Stripped finally to the 'bare essentials'
he had achieved a 'luminous simplicity'.
Removing one by one the layers of all that was 'superfluous',
down to the 'hard core',
divested of all 'attributes',
aspiring to a 'simple idea',
he strived to 're-define reality'.

Simplification, his aim, was a mere pose, we said.
Therefore, we concluded, he lied.
And yet, to him this pose was how he saw himself.
This was how he was …
He saw himself engrossed in, obsessed even
by the 'process of simplification', or 'self-simplification'.
What did this 'mean'? What did it mean to him, to us?
To him it meant arriving, through this process,
at some simple 'truth', a 'unit'
that could not possibly be simplified any further.
But this was vague—or so it seemed to us.
To us, 'simplification' meant, really, a dangerous, a suspect
obsessive drive to 'reduce' things, himself,
to what we called, in a derogatory sense, 'over-simplification'.
That is, to us it meant, again, lying of sorts. To him?
The fact is he believed in this 'good', whereas we didn't.
We neither 'believed' nor understood what 'good' means.

STEPHEN COX *Tondo: Beyond,* 1980

THE DEFINITION OF THE BEAUTIFUL

Beginning with his emotions, the causes of his emotions,
he would calculate, slowly and carefully, the weight of attributes,
the intensity and duration in him of events and situations, their tonal values.
He believed in 'purity' and he believed that one achieves purity finally
only through analysis, through a critical and analytic investigation.
He did not believe that this method diluted or diminished at all the beauty
        that accompanied his emotion.
He was certain of that.
His 'purity', he said, was the 'essence', the kernel, of the true and the beautiful.
And being a good student of the idealists, he believed
in the unique role of the imagination in his analyses,
and it only irritated him that, in his language,
people always confused 'imagination' and 'fantasy',
two altogether different notions,
which explained why so much bad poetry was written.

To us, of course, all this was either self-contradictory, or mere rationalization,
        perhaps even evidence
of his insufficient mastery of the language.
He believed, for one thing, in the indivisibility of cause and effect
and also in the essential difference between reason and emotion.
As for the 'imagination', we naturally believed that it wasn't really much different
        from 'fantasy';
such distinctions, we thought, were just foolish hair-splitting.
We thought that he had just confused things,
that his thinking was imprecise, misled by typical idealist confusion.

MARTIN MALONEY
Handsome Greek Poet – Cat Lover, 2006

Besides, all this pretended investigation regarding the definition of the 'beautiful'
did not concern us at all, such pseudo-philosophical hot air.
Because the 'beautiful' is naturally that which moves us, which acts on us through
feeling:
man, things, events and situations either in themselves, or as reflections of ideas.
Not for him, however, to accept our self-evident views.
He was irrelevant, a stranger to everyday reality.
Not only the manner of his thinking, his whole mode of life,
even his way of expressing himself were contemptible.
And if at least his poetry overcame such irritating weaknesses,
if there was a little life in his meagre work, which inspired, moved,
instructed, urged—
But no, nothing. He'd still stubbornly insist that poetry was beyond all this.

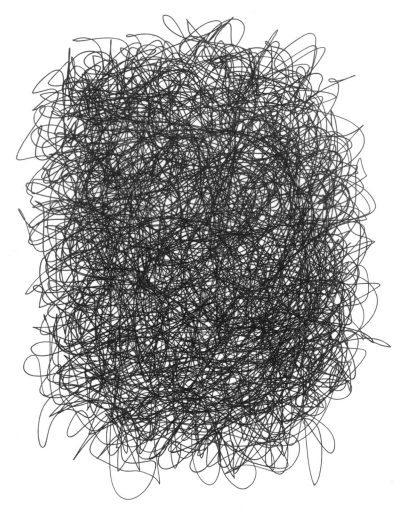

TIM HEAD *Drawing for Nikos*, 2006

FICTIVE GRAMMAR

The end? He asked. Yes, the end.
Perhaps even the ultimate finality, the ultimate, I insisted.
But to remain open, to create space without restrictions—
isn't this why we exclude?
And yet, we say, and yet.

And yet, I feel tonight such distances between us.
Now you have started new time-tables,
You are preoccupied by new principles of thought,
you apply new methods,
you map new courses on new maps.
The foliage, the illuminations, the signs keep changing.

The wisdom you crave for is, I think, a new science:
it wills to rule over all the other sciences by which we say
we acquire knowledge,
            imagination, words, language.
You resist the temptation of metaphysics, of ultimate explanations.
You want this science to be empirical, but also catholic,
a system of classification culminating in words,
the transparency of words which allows one to see, as if under glass,
the meanings that support them, that give them structure.

The voices of children repeating the unintelligible, your 'foreign' phrases,
are a litany of the winter light now,
they surround me so that distances double,
multiply to the point perhaps of final, ultimate alienation.

LISA MILROY *Light Bulb*, 1988

FICTIVE NATIONS

You have invented a name for your nation
Which pretends to represent and analyse reality
By making arbitrary choices of misleading traits
And from these traits a system.

You transform fraudulently symbolic systems which do not exist,
The wisdom of others, made-up word games,
And you transcribe obscure histories,
Heroic feats of eclipses.

And you deny even the moonlight,
Welcoming vast regions of darkness
Where even the faintest ray of light would transform
What we had hoped for into the object of knowledge.

This is how you aim to subvert common interpretations,
By paraphrasing texts which do not suit your interests,
By imposing censorship on light
In those dark regions which would be only

Meaningless representations in the imagination.

R. B. KITAJ
Smyrna Greek (Nikos), 1976–77

FACTS, FICTIONS AND FORECASTS

There was no answer. Your calling only created the expectation in you for an answer. You simply thought you had called. It would have been the same had you walked down a passage at the end of which you half-imagined to find a large dark room, the corridor being just a sort of springboard off which you would jump into a pool below, although you knew perfectly well it was impossible to tell whether what was below was a pool or a large empty room, deep, deeper still, at the very end of the corridor. (You repeat yourself: deep, deeper still, at the very end of the corridor, not in an impasse but in a corridor open at both ends.)

(The changing light: it is clear, clear, clear.)

Your pleading call remained inside you, in this finally undefined space, never addressed to anyone out there. If there was to be an answer at all it would have to come from inside that space. So you jumped: sink or swim. Your feet touched the bottom. You pushed hard and moved towards the surface again.

Miserable you moved in and out of rooms. This would have to come to an end, you said. The shock of events. No action. No continuous lines. Sometimes they seem to mark a beginning and an end but they don't really because there is nothing in between. Points at a distance. Momentary events only of a certain imperceptible duration, or even of no duration at all. Events which may or may not have happened before, after or at present. You could not ask when will it end? Or when will it begin? You knew perfectly well that causal explanations would lead you nowhere.

MAGGI HAMBLING *Wave Breaking, June (I)*, 2006

But memory? Memory of events. Memory of states. Memory of actions, of you? The memory of you at one particular moment, at another particular moment, at a third particular moment. Each moment is differentiated. A different face appears at each moment and the one is in no way related to the other. Perhaps you were not. A different face appeared each time, a different stranger. No entities of being in time. No being. Apparitions which may or may not be repeated.

(That night I heard that the words would become coherent language in your ears as you sat near the sea listening intently. You have a bent for abstractions when you forget how to express yourself. Later, your absence. You could not possibly have been here. This was as certain as your not being here at this moment. And yet we had made plans when we thought, running through—why should I go through all this again now? We had stood on the pier, our bodies reflecting the pale honey transparency of the sunset. Beyond the pier beyond the sea, on a hill, which I see now for the first time, white houses reflect the sea and are reflected in it, now as then without you here. But this is not your memory. I can try, it is possible to try to reach out to you, but I know I shall not succeed. Beyond the hill with the houses, the mountain looms high. It changes colours. The sea sometimes roars and the wind pierces the waves as they rise. It could not have been you in this same place, it could not have been me even, it could not have been me afraid to disturb your 'innocent' sleep. Your arriving and departing both having exactly the same degree of absence and later your presence was a torture. I, in anticipation, had carefully prepared for, planned in every detail, and when you were present I prepared for you. It is becoming dark now and your shape is becoming less and less distinguishable in the dark shadows. I moved as if to reach for and grasp your hand but I stop because it may not be you, surely, will not be you. Your memory then? The unforgivable moment of giving without taking. You stood at dawn on the hill. The prophesies were all wrong then? You would win? Would you finally

JOEL SHAPIRO *For Nikos*, 2006

break through these fragments of memory, unfinished love stories,
the sound barrier of birds praying to the rising sun emerging victorious.
And would you never draw back from the waves which crashed on your
legs resting on the whitesheeted rocks? Expectation was raw at that time
of the deadly white morning and you, victorious, set the whole region
on fire with your wild laughter. The prophesies were right after all,
as always.)

And consequences? Why this consequence and not that? Why this
particular series of events related in this particular order and not that?
Give me one reason. Fragments, then. Not even that. Fragments of what,
which might have been a whole before? When will it end? You persist
in asking. It will never end.

You get a feeling, a chill, of the approaching painful but quick end,
all the same. You are afraid of pain. But pain is being made to explode
inside you and soon you will learn the 'meaning' you have been so
embarrassingly and childishly craving for. Children will point at you
as if identifying an object. And then maybe there will be a fresh alert.
And there we are where we were not a moment ago.

Or nothing all the time and then, although it should have been certain,
even absolutely certain, into nothing again. A new start perhaps
among pieces of furniture like ships, in the dark, among utensils,
lamps, equipment, always into nothing, arriving at the same terminal:
the foundation of a new start, the very foundation of a new edifice which
you hope will not sink into total darkness, will not be engulfed like the
previous one, in the abyss of fears, dangers and anxieties, that edifice
which you had raised with your own hands, into which you had invested
all your life, trying to support it in mid-air with your breath, praying
it would not collapse under the weight, the tension, the stress
of the materials. You had believed it stood on absolute certainty.

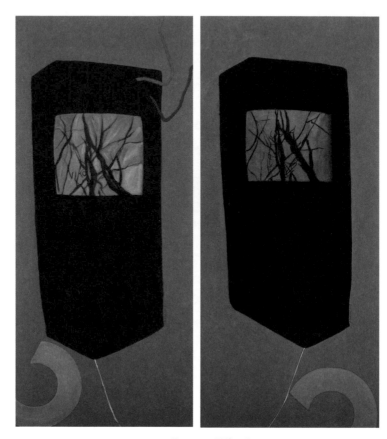

VASSO KYRIAKI *Homage to Nikos Stangos,* 2004

(The sun rays pierce the grey clouds and fall hit and break on the green surface of the sea. Imperceptibly, the park is becoming green again, the rocks take on a green tint. We can hear the distant barking of dogs playing, the distant sound of a football game, the distant car horns. Buildings too seem distant and dead, a child is crying, a woman is shouting, a singer is singing, a man stands up and looks at the horizon, the football freezes in mid-air, the voices crystallize, the players become their photograph. The light changes. The buildings now seem to be in total ruin and reconstruction seems to be going on everywhere. The trees are growing again. The open door of an old church reveals the inside which reflects a bright red and blue. A train whistles. No matter how careful we try to be there is no doubt that this light will contribute to the ruin, our ruin, confirming all the fears and anxieties, the sudden incomprehensible impatience, the bad premonitions of bad dreams. The pillow is humid with perspiration from your neck. You are betrayed by the uncertain movement of your closed eyes which all the same observe carefully. Patience too has limits.)

The title is taken from Nelson Goodman's Fact, Fiction and Forecast.

HOW COULD SPEECH EXHAUST THE MEANING OF SPEECH?

The platitudes of truth—
That was the beginning.
Now we can only turn back to
Deceiving words, the first ones,

Their acts and objects
Pacts of symbolic exchange,
The most commonplace facts
That lucid writers glorified.

Certainty was constantly
Renewing itself, feeding on
The only knowledge:
That that was the way.
A most transparent truth
Its domination over the real
Capable of annihilating it
Like him, born of pain.

Ah, the deceiving light
Suddenly like him, born of light,
The fact that merely dazzles
And takes its place out of necessity.

You sat smiling
Spoken to rather than speaking
Turned against the good,
A false renunciation.

And where is truth,
The meaning which goes unrecognized?
A closed circuit locked in
Ceremonial lies, obsessions at night.

Present speech—the monologue that activates the actor:
The birth of truth is speech
Neither true nor false
Imaginary or real.

Tonight's discourse is
A recitation in high voice
Produced before an audience—
Mass inertia.

It made up history
And it is like an indirect quotation:
The chorus on the stage and the spectators'
Language emulate the truth of revelation,

Promises of a future, of reality,
Questions of recollection
Against promises about the future:
The proof, the turning point, the theorem

Through which we guide our steps
From month to month,
The hidden objects,
The act that is an act of history, or

Falsehood, a sacred lie,
What has been written down.

JOE TILSON *Delphic Oracle*, 1980

I do not know which history, or
What meaning is now reestablished,
Common wisdom proclaimed that every age
Had found its own philosopher.
Our recent past though has revealed
This to be mere speculation, without dignity.

Your words bear witness now,
This turning aside from reason
In the domain of pure language,
Submitting to ambiguities.

What is this place?
Here imagination is the monarch
In his brilliant robes,
Rules of marble spaces

Where what appears is false
And what is false is truth,
The light changing direction
As usual revealing and concealing.

Your hero is a retarded child,
The master of relations,
Who studies in his gloomy space
Future catastrophes, decaying words.

This place is empty.
What is going on?
We want the meaning that eludes
In such heroic impersonations.

FRANK AUERBACH *Ruth Bromberg Seated*, 1992

Come close, come close.
Unwillingly we run away.
Night gathers, gathers,
Icy winds whirl, whirl.

A large body cut in fragments, freshly butchered
Is floating horizontally towards us,
Its wounds dripping deep red
Denials, fresh flesh food.

'There, there, thousands
Of infants, in their swaddling clothes
Float by, a knife plunged deeply
Into each infant bosom.'

This is, you say, how language functions.
Can we convince ourselves of the necessity
For such spiritual catastrophe?
We are the prisoners of a closed circuit.

Back to the function of the words:
The void that speaks words
When finally the day of destruction
Will arrive, glorious in its conceit,

And instrument of healing or
Of search in words uttered as words
Within ourselves and giving speech to void
In suspect words when silence fails—

ANTHONY CARO
Cubic Piece 'Letter of Introduction', 1992

This is the ritual of murder,
An appeal to truth
Through which other appeals
Will find—or they think find—a faltering expression.
Hopeless mirages, fantasies, deceptions,
The silence spoken by the void that speaks
In tongues with borrowed words.
The artifice complete.

Such gifts which are condemned to fiction,
Narrations of sleepwalkers, moments
Which look like secretive encounters
Are the birth of what we think is truth expressed in words.

The testimony of reality is heard
Invoking past ambitions, making choices
Which charter the domain
Of false and glittering transactions.

Inscriptions are deciphered, traces read,
Their meanings growing out of longings
For love, closeness, forgiveness,
Only symbolic isolations will remain, as memories.

The structure of a sentence
In our sight, a dark, fleeting reality
And also an obsession
With meanings that resist all change.

JULIAN LETHBRIDGE *Lines for Nikos,* 2006

Regression, repetition, rhetoric,
Seductive metaphors sought in a dream,
The object of desire the single phrase
Which will contain all meanings.

What we were taught were double meanings,
Unstructured texts of deep symbolic lineage,
Symptoms of language with split figures,
Ambiguous numbers that conceal the real.

Secrets then gleam in their masked words
When deceit dazzles with its forgeries,
The lucid writers hiding their laws,
Authors of phantom books of random choices.

And we in our innocence, curiously to learn,
Murmuring syllables we think reveal bright actions,
Crave for a language that belongs alone to language,
Speech that enunciates such longings but does not replace them.

We think we've forged symbolic pacts with language,
Creators of a world of words taken for things,
Legible structures of incestuous marriages
Of images in words, of the one truth.

The stanza in inverted commas is from the poem 'Το φασμα'
by Andreas Kalvos (1792–1869), translated by Nikos Stangos

THE NECESSITIES OF THE MIND

Necessities shone in the cold light
Then with words and words
In an unknown language, his.

Or he thought they shone.
He did not even think, he said.
This is what he wanted.

Decisions were unfinished
Sentences, the way he had
Of leaving things behind him.

A stranger, from another place.
This was his excuse,
The fire whose flames

Were flames of his ambition
And his desire to entrap
The unfolding mind.

And if a stranger, from another place,
Decisions would be then—
Continually, continually he wanted—

He wanted words on words,
Performances of love,
Murders of innocence,

Advice, threats and elucidations
Of the final love,
A celebration with no images.

Touch, colour, taste dissolved
In haze, a special light,
The light of endless lyricisms:

Mouth upon mouth,
Eyes on eyes,
Bodies on bodies.

If then, then the elucidation
Not of hard objects in cold light,
Not of decisions, but of proclamations,

Of a rhetoric of sighs,
Not a false rhetoric, but of appeals
To the revealing light not to reveal

A universe of images,
Glass, crystal, water,
Whose boundaries are confused.
They are body-less,
They are the truth.

BARRY FLANAGAN *House in Umbria*, 1974

ENCHANTMENTS OF THE OBVIOUS

I

Our house is invisible.
Its light is unique to it:
Its light is our eyes,
An attribute that makes it
Our invention, which others may be unaware of.
Its other attributes are:
The whispers, sighs, sobs, laughter
That are unique to us.
It is tolerant and ingenious,
Accommodating all our infirmities, all our intangibles.
It is a metaphor for us.
To others it has no meaning.
Our house is a liturgy: it invokes,
It appeals, it strives to transform us,
To make us good.
Our house confirms us. We love our appointed places in it.
And it defines us as one.

II

The trees of our land are the witnesses.
They survive so far.
You are upset by their diseases, but they win,
Not you. They are resigned.
They make greater efforts than we do;
We are fickle. They submit to the recurrent
Seasons with pleasure. They also improvise.
They wait and wait. They conceal and open up.
They move near to us when we are calm and they

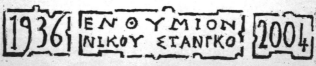

THE TREES OF OUR LAND

The Trees of our land are the witnesses.
They survive so far. You are upset by
their diseases, but They win, Not you.
They are resigned. They make greater efforts.
Than we do, We are fickle. They Submit.
to The recurrent   Seasons with
pleasure.   They also
Improvise.   They wait
and wait.   They conceal
and open up   They move near
to us when   we are calm.
and They Withdraw   from our
agitations.   Our trees
move us.   They are so
versatile   They will
not allow   us to
forget the   Shapes
They   Contain.
They are always there. Their death is terrible.

1936 ΕΝΘΥΜΙΟΝ ΝΙΚΟΥ ΣΤΑΓΓΚΟ 2004

JOHN CRAXTON 'The Trees of Our Land', 2007

Withdraw from our agitations.
Our trees move us. They are so versatile.
They will not allow us to forget the shapes they contain.
They are always there. Their death is terrible.

III

Our landscape follows regularities, it takes its course.
Its desires are always fulfilled; ours not.
And yet it is we who take things for granted
Despite our resolutions to be—patient, good?
We expect the light and it arrives
In infinite variations, in subtle colours;
It is patient, *it* is good. We are presumptuous.

But in our twilight,
When shapes and colours are their own,
We get perhaps a glimpse,
Through the abundance of fecundities
In which nothing is given though so much is given,
Of the mystifying realities.

IV

Most of our animals have been driven away.
Oh, if only we could conjure them back.
We love our animals. They make us better.
But we have tormented them unbearably.
Only their eyes remain,
And weep. We are terrible.

ROBERT BECHTLE *The View from the House, Paros,* 1989

V

Our weather is a constant surprise to me but not to anyone else.
The valley and stream mirror it. To me it is a mystery
That no forecasts will explain.
Veils of clouds slowly unfold down from its hills
And surround you, an image of you I love.
You smile.
I think you are amused by my confusion.
Your body flutters sometimes when we sleep.
I try to hold you.
That is when I think that perhaps you
Know the secret of the weather.

VI

Liguria is part of our character:
Stephen's secret visits, his photographs of us in the olive grove,
Those sunsets,
Those fireflies in the woods at night between Zoagli and Sant'Andrea,
Those mornings;
Our economies,
Your first Greek poem and my first Italian set to old tunes on our way to the sea,
Our making love in the bushes.
All this is now part of one common character,
This new person whom we have evolved from us, our new friend.
This is our Liguria, though connected to the past
By Nietzsche, Wagner, Ezra Pound, D. H. Lawrence, Adrian Stokes,
Who enrich our present,
Now our past,
In our new friend.

TIMOTHY HYMAN (*My recollecting now, seeing through my blindness ...*), 2006

VII

Often, when I am alone,
I imagine you, or, in this case, remember you, there
In that indescribable light—
Our house, the trees, the weather
Surrounding you, your aura.
My recollecting now, seeing through my blindness, comes from your image,
your isolated image, in which I search as in a photograph for a clue to my
recollection.
Words, shining examples of meaning, a sense of understanding
how words work—
And with such ease decisions are made, resolutions, elaborations,
without uncertainty,
Towards an end,
With pleasure in the elaborations, with pleasure in the open-ended structures,
with pleasure in the purposeful, meandering conclusions.
No wonder, then, we understand in retrospect.
And then these shining clarities you love so much
Emerge, unfold, proclaim in one loud chorus, their reality.

THE FAMILIAR SURROUNDINGS
OF THE WORDS

THE TYRANNY OF DISTANCES

The forbidden unfolds
Suspension rules.

Sometimes the then is concealed, sometimes it eludes.
Never the then.

It is always late, late always.
My actions accuse me, but I am unrepentant.

No word from the others.
Their silence signals. They have lost their faith.

Their modest occupations wrap them.
They defend themselves justly.

They will not allow me.
And if they do it will be late.

And so the unaccomplished will remains unaccomplished,
Plans will be formless,

Uncertainty will be their neutral light,
Opinions will run their prescribed course,

Denials will burst spectacularly into flames,
Injustice will be a support.

They will be sitting in a space,
Crowned, smiling.

The Clarity of Distances

He didn't know what to do.
The words glowed
Like crystal.

He kept repeating: the opening, the opening,
A frozen litany in the frozen light.
He thrashed.

I look at you, I surround you with love, with prayers.
I don't need to interpret you:
'The world become perfect through "love"'.

JAKE TILSON *'The Clarity of Distances'* – An Excerpt, 2006

THE CLARITY OF DISTANCES

He didn't know what to do.
The words, the phrases glowed,
Then were crystals.

He kept repeating: the opening, the opening,
A frozen litany in the sharp light.
He thrashed.

I look at you, I surround you with meanings.
I don't need to interpret you:
'The world becomes perfect through "love".'

Perception and knowledge are one.
There is this, there is this, there is this.
Inside, the early morning light in purest screens.

You are travelling alone in your distances.
I silently confirm the survival of our trophies.
There is the quiet light: it reveals and transforms.

Outside, I try to match things as they are today with yesterday's:
The weather, the light, the green, the noises and the flights of birds.
Their regularity is a quiescence.

Words are an ostentation.
Their choice is made but they will not succumb.
Images keep their place.

JENNIFER BARTLETT *'We used to say that distances define.*
Today the weather changed, I miss your light', 2006

The genuine invades,
It is the truth,
It needs no formulations.

He thought others possessed secrets kept from him:
Schoolfriends who could solve problems in geometry,
Philosophers, logicians, poets.

He thought he was condemned not to perceive or understand.
Perception and knowledge were not one.
This is a way of telling you the truth.

I want my landscape to be seen in the sharp light,
The ultimate clarification, the essential metaphor,
The 'essential' and the 'central' poem.

We used to say that distances define.
Today the weather changed, I miss your light.

THE ENCHANTMENT OF DISTANCES

Infinite, distant, pale,
Surprising distances of light, your touch.

Itineraries of your thoughts in a dark room,
The invocations of the impenetrable far.

The light hammers outside, it forges tools.
You are the interior traveller, the erotic emperor.

ANGELICA GARNETT *Untitled*, 2006

You comprehend through fictions, your true facts,
Your coronation is a brilliant spectacle.

Today you make another day, another day.
The labyrinth postpones receding vistas,

It multiplies the green
In ever-paler screens of green.

I am envious, I want to call you back.
We go into the dark.

Miracles happen in delirious light.
Distances then diminish to a bright, insistent spot,

And then the crystal of your dream is this:
Your hand that reaches out to a glass of crystal water.

THE REALM OF DISTANCES

You used to say that distances defined,
Ever-receding planes of palest green.
We tried to learn, the music would not flow.

Of distances, he thought that they defined;
The definitions were a wreck, the house burned down.
We tried to invent a plot, a mindless entertainment

Which would conceal ambition, like a field.
Orphans, we needed your support, the nurturing essence
And we failed.

BRIDGET RILEY *Large Fragment,* 2006

There were two choices:
That which seemed more appealing,
The bright metaphor that lied;

The other that concealed and was 'good'.
Define the distance and its easy glow,
The imagined glow that changes colours as you wish.

The light transforms the landscape, like a set:
Now mysteries invade the hum of our invented domes and choirs,
And now the clouds spill over in our fields and burn like metaphors.

I use your language to conceal the truth,
Hoping it is concealed
And hoping, hoping it will sound like mine.

Fire must be fed, like metaphors.
Return now to the plot, accumulating text on text,
Your supreme comfort, your escape.

Distances served your purpose, you were emperor,
Your robes, your crown, a triumph,
Proofs of order.

Rituals were prescribed.
Your rule ruled the extinction of all vaguenesses,
The avoidance of fluidities, fruitions.

You were strict.
You imposed the tyranny of distances, you won,
Your sense of order fixed the distances in frames,

TIMOTHY HYMAN (*Outside, I try to match things as they are today with yesterday's*) (*I miss your light*), 2006

Transforming them into harmless pictures on the wall:
A cherry tree that dies each spring,
Its fruit deformed, a colony of worms;

Her wrinkled hands dry skin with rings;
Her pale green dresses withered;
Meanings like jewels in her rooms.

A garden overgrown, and empty house,
Light moving slowly, softly through its rooms.
All safe now.

These are dead, empty images, they're safe,
Easy projections, then you weep.
The rhetoric of sorrow is a fraud.

Proximities are vague, they multiply:
Your hand that reaches out bursts into flames,
But it is an abstraction, like a hand.

Your body is a form, it changes form;
That too is an abstraction, undefined.
Whose hand I hold, whose body I embrace?

I am frightened of the vague.
It might engulf me in warm fluidities,
The endlessly receding images of the vague.

These mirrors mean, the engulfing green,
The loss of my reflection in their depths.
Proximities are vague and the fixed meaning lost.

THE MENTAL SPACE
LEFT BY THE
REDUCTION OF OUR
NEEDS IS TAKEN UP
BY THOSE TALENTS
ARTISTIC, POETIC
AND SCIENTIFIC,
WHICH MULTIPLY
AND TAKE DEEP
ROOT. THEY
BECOME THE TRUE
NEEDS OF SOCIETY
THEY SPRING FROM
A A NECESSITY TO
PRODUCE AND NOT
FROM A NECESSITY
TO CONSUME.

LIAM GILLICK *Swimming*, 2006

I want the meaning to be one.
Meaning is one when distances define.
Then I can talk with ease of meaning and meaning's ornament.

Ornament is the imagined glow of the harmless metaphor.
You are your illustration.
I am mine.

THE SPACE OF DISTANCES

He said our words were mirrors of our words
And this defined us, lit the appointed place;
Meaning was one.
The enchantment of enclosures was defined:
A walled-in garden where you ruled;
Your public man was you in brilliant robes.

You crowned yourself in mysteries of light,
Your served your tyrannies of green,
You changed the costumes of your metaphor, you judged.

I illustrate your body and our love,
Victims of bondage painted on a wall,
With golden frames to keep the outside out.

We sit inside an enclosure which excludes,
We overcome engulfing fears,
We are our dynasty.

Imagined space is safe.
In it, our words burst into fruit,
Ripe plums roll on the grass.

LISA MILROY *Searching Geisha*, 2003

You say that meanings are revealed
By the surroundings of the words,
Their space familiar, as we rule.

We look outside, the wilderness sustains interior orders,
Our definitions nurtured by the undefined:
Its green confirms the real, imagined green.

More than sustains, it makes the possible and true,
It tells us what they are, these willed enclosures of the light,
These greens, these marbled definitions of the mind.

Our silent garden listens to the melodies, the hum,
That are the breeze of distant choirs;
Its meaning is in listening, the purpose of the music to be heard.

We think, we imagine we are there,
That we have wandered, free at last
Into the distant source of music, light and green.

The distant source of music, light and green
Is what we say we hear, we see, when we dream.
He said our claim was fraudulent, a fake.
Another phantom mirror of the mind,
A base ambition veiled in faint, cool greens,
A waving of the hand as if, as if.

And in this dream we held
Bright, insubstantial objects
With no shape

That burned like fireflies
In a room where sighs and embraces
Were the fixtures of our dream.

We held each other lightly, we explored
The uncommitted definitions of a bond.
The light, the shapes, the sounds, the observant greens

Were uncommitted repetitions mimicking the green.
The real was undefined and uncontrolled,
A challenge to forsake the appointed place.

As if, as if held us in our enclosed, safe paradise
Which, nurtured, grew gigantic wings of green
To shield us from the undefined outside.

We looked through leaves and fruit
Silver with light, taking no risks,
At thrilling actions in the theatre outside

Where fears and fantasies were bursting into flames,
Wild in wild freedom, wonderful.
Is this how knowledge is acquired?

And then, safe, playing our enchanted roles,
Was this how ignorance was nurtured
On that fruit, the magic breast?

And is the poem a venture or a pause,
The distant, thrilling green, or is it distances denied?
What did you represent? Or were you there?

JULIAN BELL *The Waiting Room,* 1997/2007

ACCUMULATION OF TEXTS

If you were the personification—the personification only—
Of ideas, oneiric events, justifications, rationalizations,
Of unfounded fears and unacceptable actions

Then you would have no objective reality, no existence. You would
be nothing but the fiction I felt compelled to invent, a phantom.

Is this perhaps how I destroy you?
This is, then, how I destroy you, perhaps.

What is it that makes me constantly deny you and re-create you?
If it is I who invents, cultivates and imposes all the roles you play,
If I re-create you according to my own rules and needs, in my own image,
Then you are nothing more than my phantom, internal lover.

What need transforms you into a screen?

If I deny you, why then do I transform you into the phantom, internal lover?
Who imposes what?
My idea of you,
Which, perhaps, I am afraid often has no connection with you,
Makes me use you
In order to personify the roles I create for you.
You become their actor.

The week has gone; the momentary shifts and transformations have
devoured it; nothing left now but the fragments of its moments:
they multiply in layers of frightful fears: and if, and if, and if.

What if the roles I had imposed on you denied you, and their sum total did
not add up to you, were not even your representation? What do artists and
philosophers have to do with you? What does your representation proclaim?

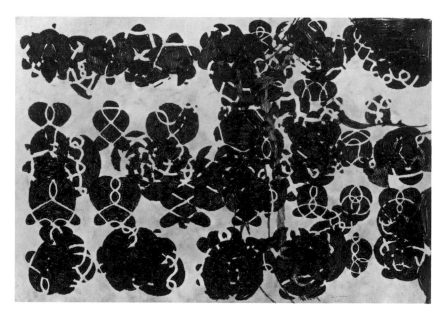

TERRY WINTERS *Untitled*, 2005

The meaning is one now, it is another now.
I repeat your movements, I repeat my own movements.
The repetitions accumulate, they are not static.

I have to start again.
We stood that morning facing each other; we were as one. The light,
the colours, the solidity of the white walls, the plum tree, the olive trees
and the vines were the natural setting for a new beginning. You were
you, I was I. We were simply surrounded by events. Later we made love;
we *were* one. And then—was it then?—the mechanism of transformation
began to move, slowly, imperceptibly. I wanted to take photographs
of you: your lips swollen from kissing, your eyes unfocussed.
You were becoming my image of you, I was becoming the image of
myself. This was the beginning of denial then. Images are phantoms,
representations, personifications, not you but your Ariel.

Why is a belief stronger than the factual evidence which disproves it?
If I believe that I am responsible for your destruction, literally or by
converting you into an image, then no proof to the contrary will make
me feel differently. Beliefs then are only the rational excuses for feelings,
they are the rich and intricate web which conceals and reveals.

HOLIDAYS

A new religion perhaps
But no time left just now
Another freedom
Love had its ways
What is it now?

Whichever way you turned
You seemed to be listening
Turning away
We had paid a great price
A generosity of spirit.

You longed for a quiet hope
The peculiar clarity of ideas
A gathering together
You could not breathe or see
You longed, sometimes.

A harmless picture in its place
In which a poem
The artificial light
A glitter which was not designed
No more than ordinary risks.

JAN HASHEY *H is for Hermes*, 1998

NEWS OF A DEATH

Have you heard?
In which a man
Then poetry
A sense of discretion
While other men act to reveal the whole.

The rest was said in silence
Always possible
The structures of life
Apathy, suicide
A monologue of peculiarities
To justify the moment.

Writing poetry
Days empty and unbearable
Having suffered
Like great lovers
I begin
A person is born
A process within himself
I had to speak of compromise.

The day would end
Had been thrown away
Killing had become a habit
And I learned to bear the pain.

In the end you said
I was seeking real clarity
The real commonplace of love
How does one know?

Good qualities
Can never be more than love or hate
If this were a crime
The right to choose
That one more day
Or one more day could come.

You have traced your life
All the curious devices
Tender affections, symbolic words
The analogy that is a special act
And you never forget
These personal symbols
Can you bear the shame
If we must endure with love or with hate
And tomorrow is still tomorrow
One of them in both
The reality known to the poets
Their own life stories.

Now you must also display not knowing
Afraid of falling
Not knowing the truth
The thought that it is conceivable to kill myself
No less than a distortion
When it is all written
As if you were dead.

A HOPEFUL DREAM

While we waited
It might not come
Their fingers twisted

He was suddenly old
His voice was uncertain
They were going away

The clocks in the valley
Giant columns
The fountains were drying

The curtain held
His friends
The city
Suicides
Like birds
Always returned

The rivers were drying
Such moments of tenderness
The search was abandoned
One day they might blossom
Summer evenings
But the animals were dead

They would not look
Embraces hurt
They would not look

Caught in the light
The fountains were dry
The fountains

Sleeping they dreamt
A place of water
Lightly.

AN OBSTACLE

All the right dates
A fleeting glance
You remain stationary
That kind of activity
A confirmation of the fact

If you always
The times I have been there
The door locked
The outside world
The only place

There is no difference
You wait then you have
Because I too waited
To become in essence your recognition
You have to believe

How important
You do things right
You want to make too many, not one
It is a dead end
Your goal is not to get somewhere

The eyes that look
No matter what
They were seen
A long time was the best time
I was lost, you looked

The outside world
Literal images to draw
My desire to look
Not only to make one but many
An excuse for seeing

Many years and no in between
One nevertheless
A natural alternative
For so many years
One place to another

For so many years no in between
I saw for the first time
And saw one place turn to another
For so many years
A natural alternative

That was the first time
The original idea
Though if I started
An image of light
The shadow changing

If I knew how
I did not want to walk away
To another absence
Too many questions
Another absence.

ELLEN PHELAN *Across the Lake*, 1996

Clearing Storm, 1996

ON A WALK

You gained by disputing it
The time came
Things of the imagination
Weather
An external event
What was happening

I did not know
One did not know
A new world was promised
Movements of life
Events

True
Not what we knew
In the mind
These are the things
Itself
The new imagination

Reading maps
Not only in the mind
These are the things
A new reality

Storm Cloud, 1996

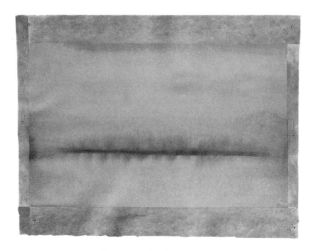

Red Dawn (Reflected), 1996

Suppose we try
Longer and longer
What is remote
The passions
The measure of the poem

Lovers of truth
Sometimes subtler
No limits
Something to do
To live our lives.

ASPASIA STASINOPOULOU *Untitled*, 1980

SPACE OF IDEAS

'I am waiting now, although I won't ever wait: the answers fold in
on themselves, slow and fast, slow and fast, their pulse eludes me.
You forget often. You remember transparently, sometimes positively,
sometimes negatively.'

That was before. Now your absence.

Texts protect. Now I want you, now I want you: sometimes I want one,
sometimes another. Distance protects. One word will do, another will do.
I want you and I appeal to others whom I deprive of their objective reality.
I escape and elude. I try not to replace you with the irreplaceable.
It is easy. Performance is not enough. Words melt. Your performance:
what does it mean? Its meaning, theatrical, contradicts the representation
of your presence, of what you are in my mind. I mean this: that you exist
now in my mind, that you 'are' only a metaphor and this 'being' is the
substitute of what was concrete before: your space, your weight, your
touch, your taste, the taste of the point between ear and neck.

You and you dissolve into one.

I refuse to illustrate you. If I did I might corrupt you. Not you yourself,
but my feelings about you. How can I bridge my conviction that I should
not illustrate you and my eagerness to proclaim you? Why do I want to
proclaim you?

This is concrete: I waited for you, now near the empty fountain, now
by the arch. It was cold. It was sunny. I was wearing my blue overcoat.
Where would you appear from? You might appear from anywhere.
Where should I have waited? You were late. I wanted you to come right
away. What would you tell me? Would I be able to master the pretended
naturalness, the nervous jokes? What was your significance, and what was
the significance of our meeting? Interpretations interfere, they invade me.

JULIAN OPIE *Abstract Composition for Nikos and David*, 1985

I don't want to express anything that would make it seem I am
illustrating you. I don't want your representation.

The texts interfere, the promises—not promises made to anyone,
but my own, internal promises.

Absence is concrete, it pursues me. I return to this again. I think I cannot
resist the attraction to the idea of absence. Had you gone? Had I perhaps
driven you away? Could you have gone because I imposed it, or maybe
in order to vacate the space which I was determined to inhabit myself,
alone, without the irritations and compromises imposed by cohabitation?

You and you and you dissolve into one. All the protagonists and all
the antagonists are only you. You are all the varieties, the variations
of the same you. And you and you and you and you and you, here and
there, before and after, then and now, before then and after then, here
absent and there absent, here before and there now. Series of syllogisms
that protect and detract, that relieve and induce calmness of absence,
not your absence now, but the absence of thought, where space is finally
empty, thinking thoughtless, its space filled perfectly by the weight,
the colour, the touch, the taste of the hard, shiny objects which
stand there, alone, still, absolute, self-possessed, not even victorious.

TO SAY TO ONESELF
SUDDENLY ONE MORNING

To say to oneself suddenly one morning
Then to open the door

Whatever remains so often there of course
No lyrical effusions in these actions
Discoveries as long as life

Through months like these
Promises are hidden or so one hopes
The mere facts exist in these loves
And I cannot remember yesterday's inner prospects

Usually more than we know is given
There is much now given, like love.

WHAT CALM THEN?

I wanted to prove to you
In what survives
That it was justified
If you compare the photograph and now
The same person only slightly coarsened

The visible features and colours
By which an earlier peace
Becoming less pronounced
Perhaps singular happiness
A kind of outward prosperity

Young men assembled with raised arms
Daffodils in the grass
Smiling through teeth
Too late to start again
Dreaming now only of what died.

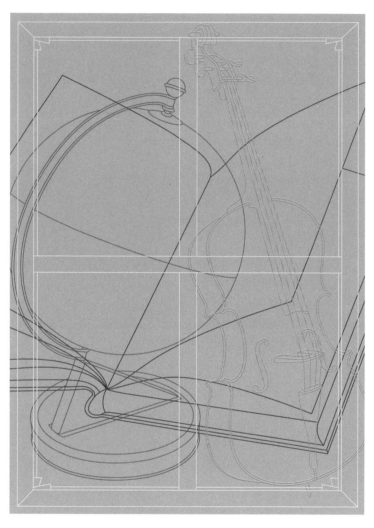

MICHAEL CRAIG-MARTIN *Montagu Square*, 2006

IMPERATIVE PRESENT

Maybe from all these fragments
The present will emerge one day which is not imperative
But simply be present,
Neither of avoidance nor task—the rules that force it to exist—
But be itself, clear and simple.
And maybe then, at another level now beyond me
Where continuity will, I hope, bring together these forced fragments,
The present will be fecund with the ideal fecundity of now.
Without the fear of misunderstanding,
Maybe these words will then communicate what is unique to their
sounds as I utter them.

MARK LANCASTER *Zapruder/Nikos/David, 1967–2006*

PURE REASON

(for David)

Your hardness or softness? Your colour, smell, weight,
your impenetrability? Your taste, sound, shape? What then?
You draw me to a series of paralogisms, but I think I know better.
It is your substance, the space you occupy in the abstract, your duration
which is independent of incidents, that I study. Your permanence.

Year after year, I try to make sense of this, the 'scandal of pure reason',
as you call it. I aim high. My aim is more than a mere theory of knowledge;
it is the whole culture of human reason, its ideals. The rules are strict: my
search, for one thing, has to be independent of experience; it has to spring
from a determination of the will. I am only allowed to make references
to you, you to me. We are, we tell ourselves, the analogies of experience.
You and I are the limits of our knowledge, we are the limits of reason.
Beyond, there is purity.

We even arrive at conclusions: 'General truths, which at the same time bear
the character of an inward necessity, must be independent of experience—
clear and certain by themselves.' How we long for them, these certainties.
How transforming they seem. How we value this very potential of
transformation, the urge, the necessity to burst beyond ourselves,
but burst beyond where any such craving would be inconceivable.

You are right, of course, when you scold me for my impatience,
my laziness, my lack of perseverance. You insist I define my terms
and you are absolutely right. You insist that I go back to the beginning
and clarify what I mean by 'pure'. I try: 'Knowledge a priori, if mixed up
with nothing empirical, is called pure.' I know I have a pure knowledge
of you, therefore. 'Necessity and strict universality are safe criteria of
knowledge a priori and are inseparable one from the other.' 'Necessary'
you are. 'Strictly universal'? If I know I have pure knowledge of you, and
necessity and strict universality are inseparable, then you must be strictly
universal as well. This is the proof.

I love your body. 'Take away, for example, from the concept of a body as supplied by experience, everything of the body that is empirical, one by one; such as colour, hardness or softness, weight and even impenetrability, and there still remains the space which the body (now entirely vanished) occupied. That you cannot take away.' I know I shall always have your space. I love your space. But I also want your colour, your hardness or softness, your weight, your impenetrability. I love your body.

We try to adhere to the strict rules we have created to remain pure. And yet, despite our strict adherence to our rules, we are at the same time immersed in and committed to a whole mass of manifestations, incidents, even 'significant events' that surround us. We are about to disobey our rules, these rules we ourselves have created.

We soon extend our references to allow more than our mere duality. The analogies of experience multiply. The limits are extended, pushed further and further away from the original claims of purity. Things, then, invade, they become metaphors, the metaphors now confused with the analogies. What really matters: you come, you go, you sit next to me, you sit next to someone else, you continue your eventful course. And so do I. We become absorbed by experience which includes the experience of each other in all its absurd details. Still, we say that these experiences are only the analogies of something else, something that is whole and contains us.

The idea of knowledge haunts us. It is our 'meaningful' obsession. We analyse, calculate, plot, we proceed by stratagems, we scheme, we circumvent, overreach, outsmart, we are crafty and artful, acute, shrewd and subtle, resourceful and ingenious. We crave so much for this knowledge we'd do anything to achieve it. It is our motor and fuel in one.

'Inspired by the splendid proof of the power of reason, the desire
to enlarge' my 'knowledge sees no limits.' You are now tired of my
infidelities. You insist the space is empty. You want to go away. You are
like 'the light dove, piercing in her easy flight the air and perceiving its
resistance, imagines that flight would be easier still in empty space'.
You leave with the determination to limit all references to yourself. You
say that I have spoiled the game by rushing things, anxious to finish our
edifice as soon as possible without making sure first of the solidity of the
foundations. You say that I kept deceiving yourself and myself, believing
foolishly as I did in the apparent solidity of our foundation. You leave and
your accusations hang in the air like an aurora borealis: I have been dealing
in simplifications and mere explanations. This was my greatest infidelity.
I suppose you must be right. I am numb in your absence.

And yet—

Tendono alla chiarità le cose oscure,
Si esauriscono i corpi in un fluire
Di tinte: queste in musiche. Svanire
È dunque la ventura delle venture.

Obscurities strain to become clarity,
Bodies dissolve in a fluidity
Of colours: these in music. Vanished
Is the chance of chances.

Tendono alla chiarità le cose oscure:
The movement of your thought,
The seaweed in the hyaline water, moving,
The correspondence of your appearance to your presence or absence,
The flowing into each other of precepts and concepts,
The frightening silence surrounding isolated sounds, us,

JOHN GOLDING *J.14 (Icebreak)*, 1990

The tangible and fluid interchange of incomprehensible clarities
when we sleep,
The inaudible sounds whose ululation dominates the cats' dreams.
And in this process, opposites, the antinomies, lose their prescribed
definition by turning into each other. Thus, sound has become silence,
silence sound, movement is now stasis, stasis movement, your
appearance is always certain when you are absent, the previously
invisible concepts are now most concretely visible, while I cannot trace
the shape, see the colour, even imagine the hardness or softness of what
used to be objects before; they elude me. And pleased as I am to have
the obscurities turned into clarities, I cannot accept now the clarities
turning turbid.

Disjunction has triumphed. Now each on our own, we muse about our
pure craving. We are moved by our fear, our shame of failure, the failure
to shape the ultimate object of our craving as fact, a fact that cannot be
made empty. The disjunction gains ground, the polarities turn away
from each other, the antinomies refuse to come together in a fruitful
conjunction. They become anarchic. We fear anarchy, for anarchy
breeds dogma. You are surrounded by your 'purity'; I am surrounded
by my 'purity'. We have failed. Each of us keeps to himself.

The seasons have lost their clarity.

But an affinity with something—some vague recollection perhaps—
conjures up this silence which makes me want to talk to you:

I think again and again of my total dedication to you, how I want all the
time to safeguard it from what, I don't know. Distance brings me nearer
to you and you become sacred. I think and talk of you as if about an
abstraction to which I am wholly committed, which, if I ever betrayed,
would be betraying everything sacred.

STEPHENIE BERGMAN *Happy Birthday Nikos*, 1975

I like this, the opportunity to conjure you up, my feelings about you, in this silence, in the abstract. The cats feel it too and they behave for the first time in days; they luxuriate in this, your calm. We all feel safe, confident. You fill us. The stillness in your room longs for you and holds you still, still in a way which physical presence makes impossible. We pause and rest in your absence which is so full of your presence, your abstraction. Words now force themselves striving for a definite end: you.

Everything here relates to you. The walls define your size, the pools of light explain your colours, the rooms are tuned to your voice, our bed admits to your weight. I sleep on your side now and I am not afraid. I feel secure and confident. I can even dream of others, your antagonists in a game of no permanent significance.

I could talk for hours. My tone of voice may be borrowed, but the voice is mine. It is true. I can tell you now, through you, due to you, I see and understand others. You provide the focus, the definition. Without you they'd fall apart, they'd become imprecise, vague, hypothetical.

I am so afraid of not seeing, of self-deception, of deception. I am afraid of banalities of thought and feeling which creep in without my realizing it. They are terrible, thin, shifty snakes. They are the greatest danger. They betray the 'moral qualities'. This is what punishment is: the exposure of the slow and creeping betrayal of moral quality. Sometimes I think that my words are nothing but a proof of this betrayal.

The bottom—fathomless before—suddenly appears at the top.

But *you* have to keep fighting. *You have to keep fighting* against this slow, creeping betrayal. You have to be prepared to sacrifice yourself in this fight. *You have to.* I need it.

Your absence defines your presence properly, it presupposes it.
The cats perk up their ears towards some hardly audible noise out in
the corridor, outside the door. When I am here alone they know that
you are not here but that your arrival is surely imminent. They certainly
believe in causal relationships in a way we consider naïve. They expect
the noises outside the door to be you and their faith in this is absolute.
The cats are constant and faithful in a way that I am not: I know the date
of your arrival and therefore I know that it is not as simple as making
the false assumption that any noise outside the door is a guarantee of
your appearance inside the room. And yet, soon, when the date of
your return does arrive, their association between the noise and your
appearance, the conjunction of these two events, will come true
and they will feel quite satisfied, their theory at long last verified.
Now the noise has stopped and the cats stretch and go to sleep,
again unperturbed by causal irregularities that do not threaten
their convictions.

I pray for you in a way you never suspect except perhaps intuitively
when we touch in sleep. I pray for you without knowing I pray, for when,
asleep myself, I hold you at night something like prayer flows from me,
surrounds you, enters you through your skin.

I have a terrible thirst to give you whatever you need, strength, will,
peace. Can you see what I mean? A thirst to emit rather than absorb,
a thirst that is turned inside out.

Sometimes you are blind to this and that is what hurts most: your
blindness to my need to give you what you probably don't need.
Then my anger blocks me, blocks all my need for you.

One by one the old uncertainties return again in this quiet without you:
the need for words, the fixed gaze, wanting to learn, to understand,

this old foolishness which is where we started from. Isolation, reinforced,
deepens: the talking to oneself, the loss of concentration, the constant
thinking that one has forgotten something very important. All the known
banalities. The banalities multiply: 'I feel empty.'

Your mechanisms are subtler, more sophisticated than mine;
they coordinate their activities towards one end. Mine are out of gear,
I think. Where one thing is expected another happens. The cats,
innocent victims, can't tell any longer when to expect affection or
cruelty, and, so deeply confused, they age overnight, then die.

The door opens. No one comes in.

We talked about you tonight. The moon is full. The buds are bursting.
What more could we wish for? Εγω δε μόνα κατεύδω … Some vague
recollection, a sudden illumination in this moonlight brings me, with
certainty, the new knowledge: you precede experience. This must be
where my calculations had gone wrong. I had never seen you this way
before. When we talked about you tonight, we were simply reaffirming
the boundaries of our faith in you. We saw what you promise. We took
account of what you have achieved: your bursting beyond experience.
We returned in full circle to the fact that can't be experienced and
proven through our senses: that you are a category of the mind;
therefore that you are beyond any need to prove.

The clarity of inward necessity, simple and certain in itself:
to make this our categorical imperative.

But can we understand this? Can we understand it in such a way
that it is not a moral dictum?

You believe in revelations.

STEPHEN BUCKLEY *Field*, 2002

Your pulse, the thumping of your heartbeat as I hold you closely,
and, around our bed, the choirs
of unison, making the curtains billow as if by some cosmic, our, breath—

Our whole beings apprehend, are aware of this inward necessity,
this revealed point
we had dreamed about without believing it possible for us. This is our love.
Once the centre is fixed we can allow the antinomies to revolve around it,
to resolve themselves as if by magic, and fabulous marriages will take
place among them.

My love, we can build our solid edifice. We can take our time,
plan it as we like, change it as we like.
We can improvise. Oh, the things we can do!
The things we may, if we wish, leave undone!

The analogies of experience dissolve now into one another,
as 'bodies dissolve in a fluidity of colours, these in music',
in the pure light of this ultimate knowledge, in this pure reason.

The quotations are from Immanuel Kant. The Italian is from 'Falsetto' by Eugenio Montale.
The Greek is from Sappho's 'I sleep alone ...'.

JASPER JOHNS *The Aim Was to Put a Poem Together*, 2006

THE AIM WAS TO PUT
A POEM TOGETHER

Or meaning even
The voices of sympathetic callers
What might be thought impersonal subjects
Or letters from someone he loved.

NOTES ON THE POETRY OF NIKOS STANGOS

Nikos's most vivid poetic sensibility was philosophical. That is, sensitivity and idea were to him one, so the concept of 'beauty', 'truth', 'the good' evoked subtle emotional reactions personal to him and personal to his poetry.

He wrote these poems in English, but I like to think the 'sense' behind them is Greek, a 'sense' that apprehends ideas as forms, forms as ideas. In his poetry, 'light' is both light as seen with great clarity and light as idea, as in the line 'I miss your light'. Concepts were to him images; images, concepts.

As much as he was a man of reason, he was a man of imagination that found expression in such images as *the light hammers outside, it forges tools*', an image inspired by his attraction to the long tradition of Greek surrealism. Yet, he distrusted imagination's unreal 'ornaments' and craved the rational 'real'.

His poetry has so much to do with 'absence', but 'absence' as potent as 'presence'.

He used the word 'antinomy', in Greek αντινομια, and in his poems worked to bring together all 'oppositions of one law to another', all 'contradictions between conclusions which seem equally logical, reasonable or necessary', and resolve them.

The dictionary definition of 'antinomy': *Philosophy*: contradiction existing between two apparently indubitable propositions.

The two great historical influences on him were: the love of freedom of Classical Greece and the love of order of Byzantium.

Philosophy was so much a part of his poetry he used the philosophical term 'categorical imperative' and gave it poetic sense, imbuing the term with such pure brightness it became its brightness more than it remained a term, and in the purity of that brightness he did resolve the antinomy of thought and feeling, making in his poetry all thought feeling, all feeling thought. To him, the brightest 'categorical imperative', the ultimate resolution of body with mind, mind with body, was 'love', that most philosophical of terms.

Because he believed in love absolute he struggled to find love's imperative, finding it, finally, as an innate category of the will to love.

As impersonal as the philosophical questions he raises – can one know reality? or, more, can one in reality know, can one love, another? – behind these questions and impelling them to answers is his most personal craving, his most personal *need*, to live, himself, a life of the greatest purity of thought and purity of feeling; and because he believed that a life most lived is lived in loving another, his poetry is most impelled by his most personal craving, his most personal *need*, to love purely, to love with total clarity and transparency, to love with the belief that love itself will reveal a new knowledge of reality.

He asked the ultimate questions in his poetry, wanting poetry to be as pure as pure reason, and in 'Pure Reason' he made the answer imperative, simply.

The influences on his poetry are varied, from Giambattista Vico
to Wallace Stevens.

Here is one of his notes for a poem:
*Or did I mistake your role for that of Scienza Nuova? Could I have put you absent-
mindedly into the wrong play? No, no, I'm sure I couldn't have made such a mistake.
But maybe I meant to force a marriage. Maybe I should have called for the New
Reason, or The Pure Science, or The Science of Purity. Or maybe that'll be the
next scenario: La Scienza Nuova. I think you'll have to be the protagonist again.*

ACKNOWLEDGMENTS

The idea of publishing a volume of Nikos Stangos's poems in English
was that of his colleague at Thames & Hudson, Andrew Brown, who
also thought of asking the artists Nikos worked with, or knew as friends,
to contribute whatever they considered appropriate to the poems they
were sent. Some artists contributed original work created especially
for this book: Jennifer Bartlett and Jake Tilson (both with words from
or adapted from 'The Clarity of Distances'), Michael Craig-Martin,
John Craxton, Liam Gillick, Tim Head, Howard Hodgkin, Timothy
Hyman, Jasper Johns (inspired by 'The Aim Was To Put A Poem
Together'), Vasso Kyriaki (in which Nikos's name is defined by
branches), Mark Lancaster, Julian Lethbridge, Andrew Lord, Martin
Maloney, and Keith Milow. The portrait of Nikos by R. B. Kitaj is the
painting *Smyrna Greek (Nikos)* in the Thyssen-Bornemisza Collection.
The sketch by David Hockney was done in 1999 on a memorandum
pad in Nikos's office at Thames & Hudson, and the camera-lucida
drawing was done in the artist's studio in the same year. The drawing
by Stephenie Bergman was done at home, with Nikos's cat. Other artists
contributed works that have personal associations with Nikos – such as
Frank Auerbach's portrait of Ruth Bromberg (Ruth being a dear friend
of Nikos's), Robert Bechtle's watercolour of a view from the terrace of
Nikos's house on the island of Paros, and Joe Tilson's work inspired
by Greece. The drawing by Barry Flanagan is of the house in the
countryside of Umbria that Nikos so loved, and which Barry did in situ.
In some cases, as that of Stephen Cox and Julian Opie, the works
illustrated here were gifts. The light bulb by Lisa Milroy was given to
Nikos by her when he was ill. All the remaining artists – Julian Bell,
Stephen Buckley, Anthony Caro, Angelica Garnett, John Golding,
Maggi Hambling, Jan Hashey, Ellen Phelan, Bridget Riley,
Joel Shapiro, Aspasia Stasinopoulou, and Terry Winters – chose works
specifically in loving memory of Nikos. All the works honour Nikos,
and are reproduced with thanks to the artists.

DAVID PLANTE

LIST OF ILLUSTRATIONS